A Fish Hatches

To Pat

Acknowledgments

The author wishes to thank Isaac Bao, research scientist
at the Osborn Laboratories of Marine Sciences, New York Aquarium,
for his helpful reading of the manuscript.
The photographer wishes to thank the following:
Cole W. Wilde, Chief,
Connecticut Department of Environmental Protection;
Joseph S. Holyst, Manager,
Burlington Hatchery, Burlington, Connecticut;
Peter J. Vernesoni, Manager,
Quinebaug Valley Hatchery, Central Village, Connecticut;
A special thanks to:
Michael Vernesoni, Manager,
Kensington Hatchery, Kensington, Connecticut, and
Leslie Corey, owner-manager,
Rainbow Lake Trout Farm, North Haven, Connecticut.

28474

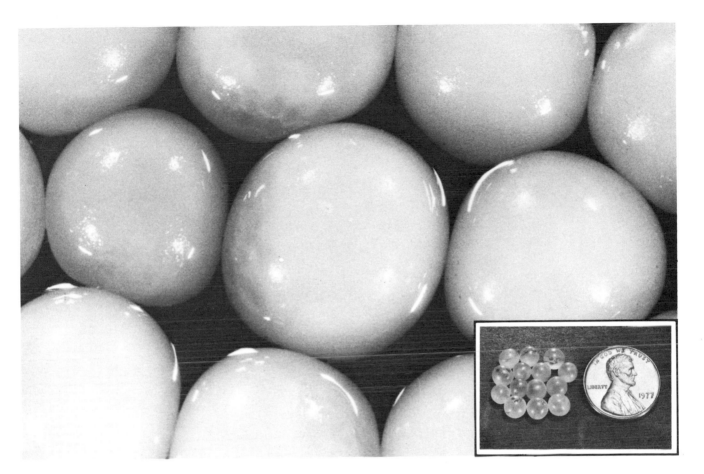

This picture shows some fresh trout eggs
that were laid only a few hours ago.
Up close they look large, don't they?

Actually, the eggs are small.
When they are placed next to a penny,
you can see their true size.
It is hard to believe that each of these eggs
may hatch a fish that can grow more than a foot long
and weigh several pounds.

In a hatchery, where trout are raised,
eggs are squeezed out of a female fish.
This is done gently and does not hurt the fish.

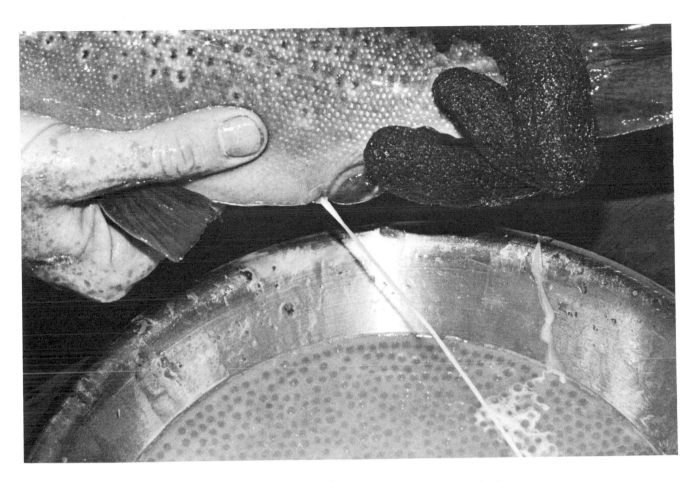

Then milt is taken from a male fish.
The milt contains sperms,
which fertilize the eggs.

The eggs are kept in a special incubator
where the temperature is just right
for the eggs to develop.

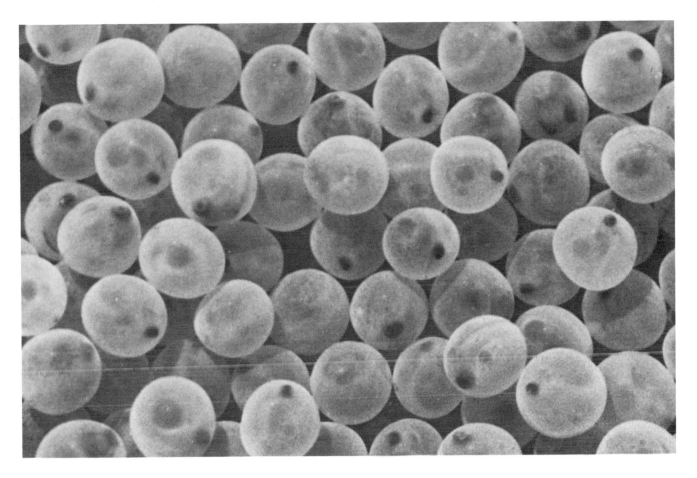

In a week or two they are called "eyed eggs."
Now you can see the fishes' eyes
through the clear walls of the eggs.
They look like dark spots.

A close-up of one egg shows the eye
and the whole body of the embryo,
or unhatched fish.
The embryos are nourished by the yolk of the egg.
They get what little oxygen they need
from the water around them.
In about two months they are ready to hatch.

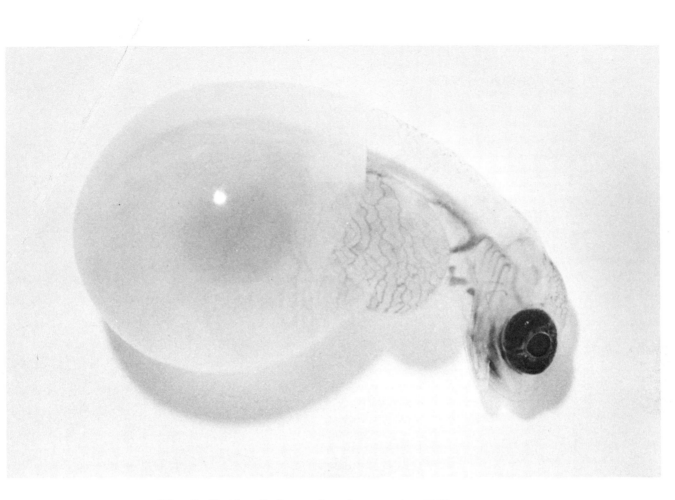

Each little fish wriggles out of the egg.
This one is coming out head first.

This one has broken out tail first.
Its head is still inside the clear egg.
Attached to the middle of the fish's body
is the round yolk sac.
Because the young fish
is still connected to the yolk sac,
it is called a "sac fry."

For the next few weeks the sac fry
does not need to eat or breathe.
It gets its food from the yolk sac.
Oxygen comes in from the water through the skin.

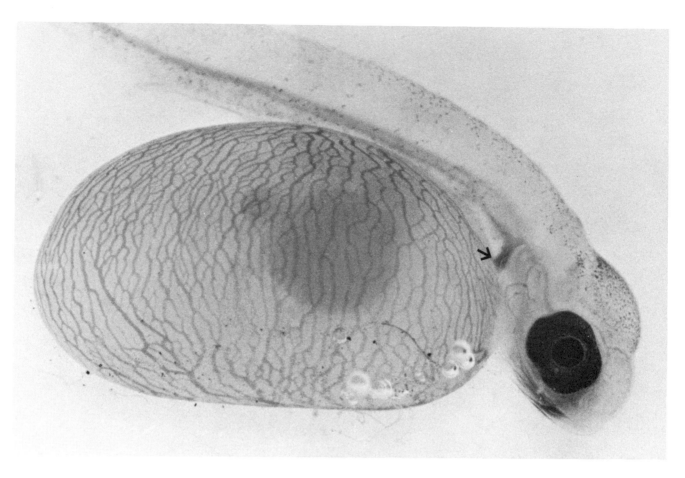

The little dark spot that the arrow
is pointing to is the heart.
The gray circle inside the yolk sac
is a drop of oil.
This oil is used as food energy by the fry.
It also serves as a buoy to help
the little fish keep its balance.

In a few days the yolk sac becomes smaller.
When the sac was very large and heavy,
it was hard for the fry to swim.
But now that the sac is smaller,
the fry begins to move about.

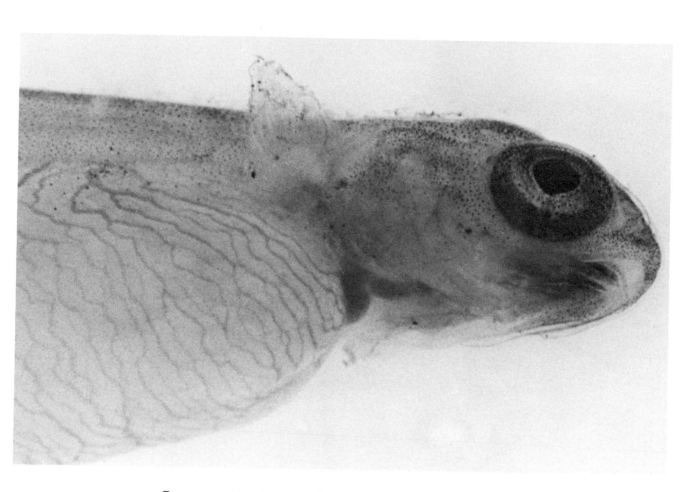

It uses its fins to help it swim.
In this picture you can see the front fin
behind the head.
It looks blurry because it is moving.

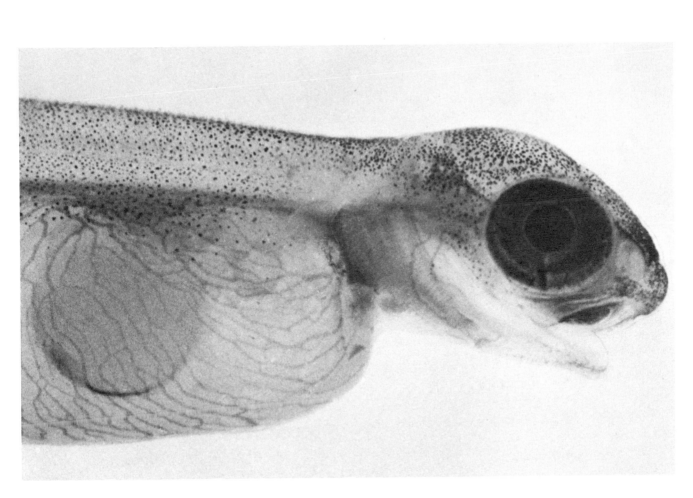

Now the mouth breaks open.

The little fry is breathing on its own.

Eventually all of the yolk sac
is drawn into the body.
The fry grow and develop
until they look like any other small fish.

The young trout has marks on its sides
that look like up-and-down bars.
These bars are called "parr marks."
They make the fish hard to see
when it is swimming through grasses.

The trout takes about three years to reach maturity.
During this time its markings change.
The adult fish does not have parr marks.
It has spots on the upper part of its body,
which help it blend with pebbles
on the bottom of a stream.

The trout has eight fins.
The large one on its back is the dorsal fin.
The one behind the dorsal fin is the adipose fin.
The powerful tail fin is the caudal fin.
The one on its belly near the tail is the anal fin.
The two in front of the anal fin are the pelvic fins.
The two behind the gills are the pectoral fins.

Can you name all the fins you see
on the fish in the picture?

A trout's body is covered with scales.
Up close you can see that the scales
overlap like shingles on a roof.
They form an armored coating
that protects the fish from injury.
The fish is also protected by a coat of slime.
The slippery coating helps the fish
slide through the water faster.

Trout feed on small animals like minnows,
insects and their larvae, worms, tadpoles,
and even frogs.
The trout's sharp little teeth are not used to chew
but to keep prey from escaping once it is caught.

Because a fish lives underwater,
it cannot get oxygen by breathing air
as land animals do.
It must get the oxygen that is dissolved in water.
To do so, the fish uses its gills.
In the picture the gill cover behind the fish's head
is being lifted, so you can see the gills.

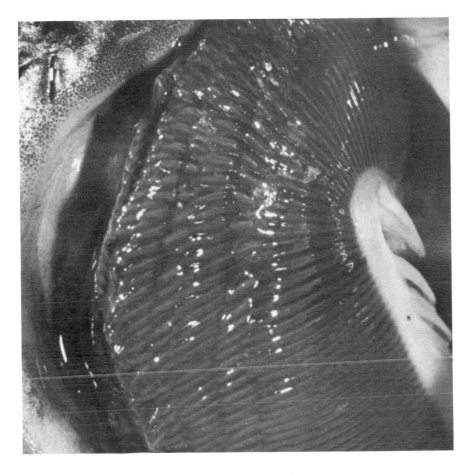

Up close you can see how the gills
are arranged in layers.
There are four gills on each side of the fish.
The bony gill rakers, seen at the right,
strain out pieces of food and trash.

Just as the man's finger passes through
the fish's mouth into the gill opening,
so water is taken into the mouth
and pushed out toward the rear of the fish.
As the water passes over the gills,
oxygen is picked up by a special substance
in the red blood cells called "hemoglobin."
This substance pulls the oxygen out of the water
and binds it to itself.
Then the oxygen is carried through
the fish's bloodstream.
The water that is pushed through the gills
moves the fish forward a little by jet propulsion.
Therefore, a fish at rest, staying in one place,
has to row backward a bit with its pectoral fins
to keep from moving forward.

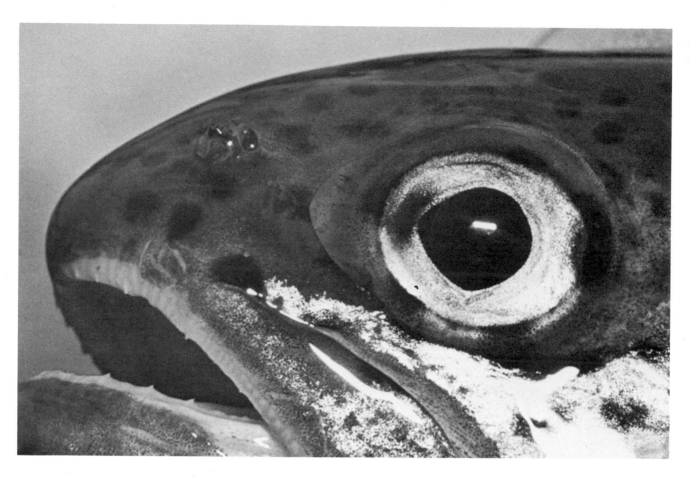

To sense the presence of prey,
the trout has keen eyesight and good color vision.
Its eyes are large and do not have eyelids.
Land animals need eyelids
to keep their eyes from drying out.
By blinking every few seconds,
the eyelids spread a film of tears over the eyes.
Fish do not need eyelids
because they are always underwater.

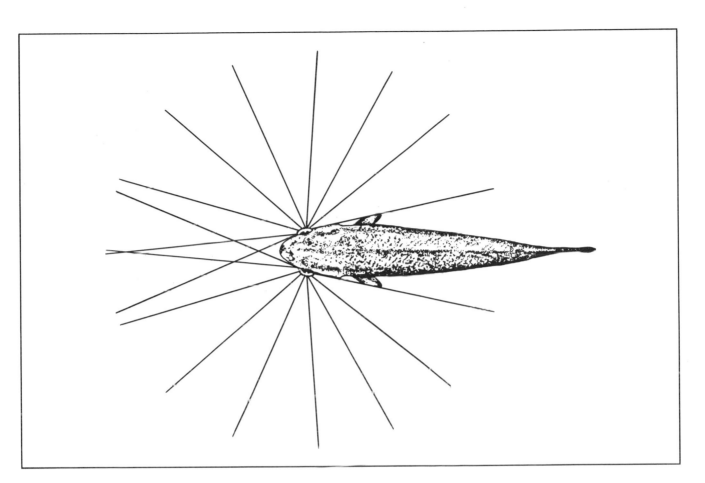

Because of the position of the eyes,
the fish can see almost in a full circle.
There is only a small blind spot
directly behind the fish.

The fish's nostrils are not used for breathing
and do not connect with the throat
as the nostrils of land animals do.
Instead, each nostril leads to an organ of smell,
which senses odors that are carried
by currents of water.

The trout has ears inside its head,
but there are no ear openings or eardrums.
Sound waves from the water are carried
through the skin, flesh, and bones of the fish's head
to the inside ear.
The trout can hear very well underwater.
It can even hear a worm wiggling on the bottom.

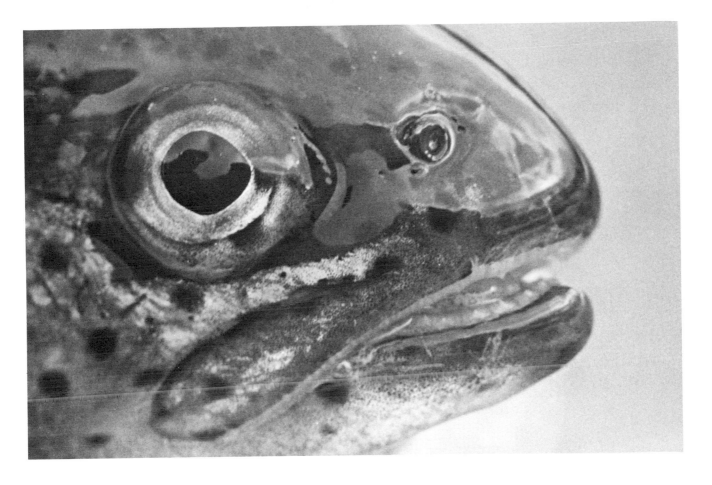

Fish have a sense that most other animals do not.
This sense is the lateral line.
Lateral means *side*, and the lateral lines
run along the sides of the fish.
In the picture the line
looks like a seam in the fish's scales.
Actually it is a tube filled with fluid
under the skin.
Special cells in the tube react
to tiny currents in the water.
A fish that has been blinded can still catch prey
by sensing its presence with the lateral lines.

Many people think that a fish
uses its fins to row itself through the water.
In fact, the fins are used mostly
for steering, balancing, and putting on the brakes.
When the trout is moving fast,
the fins are laid back into shallow slots on its body.
Then they do not get in the way
of the fish's forward movement.

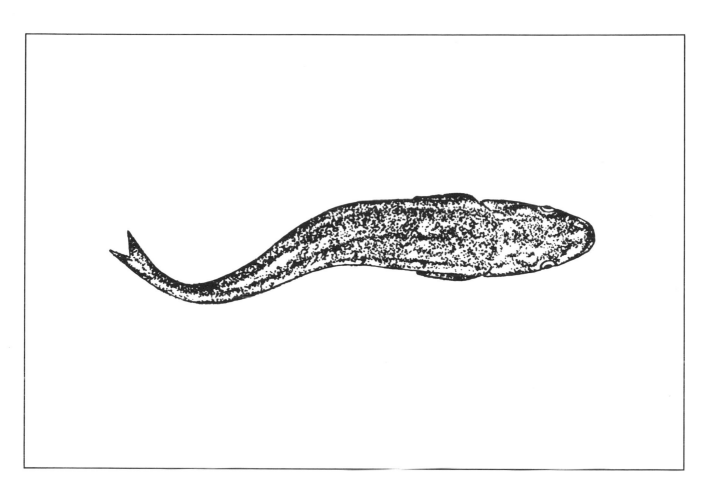

To swim fast, the fish uses its tail and its side muscles.
The powerful tail sweeps from side to side,
and muscle waves pass along the fish's sides.
Its body forms the shape of an S
as it weaves through the water.
Swimming in this way, a large trout can reach speeds
of ten miles an hour.

Often the trout lies in wait
at the bottom of a stream.
When it sees an insect floating
on the surface of the water,
it lunges up and catches the prey.
With a snap of its tail
the trout can leap high out of the water
to grab an insect or a fisherman's lure.

You can see a trout yourself
at a fish hatchery, an aquarium,
or in a lake or stream.
When you see one, you will know a lot
about how this beautiful fish lives
—from its beginnings as a tiny egg
to its maturity as a fast-swimming hunter.

Born in Newark, New Jersey, Joanna Cole grew up in East Orange. After attending the University of Massachusetts and Indiana University, she earned a B.A. degree in psychology at the City College of New York. Later she took graduate courses in elementary education at New York University and served for one year in a Brooklyn elementary school as a librarian. Mrs. Cole now is a children's book editor. She and her husband live in New York City.

Jerome Wexler was born in New York City, where he attended Pratt Institute. Later he studied at the University of Connecticut. His interest in photography started when he was in the ninth grade. After service in World War II, he worked for the State Department in Europe as a photographer. Returning to the United States, he specialized in photographing advanced farming techniques, and the pictures he made have been published throughout the world. Now his photographs of plants and animals have illustrated a number of children's books. Mr. Wexler presently lives in Wallingford, Connecticut.